Learning
Centers:
Children On Their Own

Virginia Rapport
Associate Editor

Mary N. S. W. Parker
Editorial Assistant

$2.50

The Association for Childhood Education International
3615 Wisconsin Avenue, N.W.
Washington, D.C. 20016
Third-class postage paid at Washington, D.C.

Contents

1. Personalized teaching and individualized learning   3
   Jack R. Frymier and Charles M. Galloway

2. The changing role of the teacher   16
   Vito Perrone

3. Organization for individual work   26
   David E. Day and Dwight W. Allen

4. Evaluating and recording children's activities:
   Diagnosing educational need   38
   Bill Elliott and Mary Jo Woodfin

   Children on their own—
   Centers and stations for learning   52
   Margaret Fennel and Elizabeth Kelly

5. Helpful hardware   55
   Arthur M. Enzmann

6. Those wide open spaces   66
   Gudrun Dewar

   Dimensions of freedom   74
   T. Darrell Drummond

7. Learning out of bounds   76
   Leslie P. Evans

1969-70 Annual Bulletin Order
Copyright 1970, Association for Childhood Education International
Library of Congress Catalog Number 71-133244

Personalized teaching and individualized learning

Jack R. Frymier and *Charles M. Galloway*
College of Education, The Ohio State University

1

As Johnny walked toward the entrance of his neighborhood school, he met a couple of friends on the way and they stopped to talk about the ball game they were going to play in the afternoon. Johnny had a new fielder's glove which he passed around for the boys to admire. Their conversation was animated with teasing and laughter. After a few minutes, they entered the red brick building.

Johnny went directly to his homeroom, took his seat, and put his books away in his desk. After the ritual of opening school exercises, he turned to page seventy-six in his mathematics book. The assignment was written neatly on the boards and he knew exactly what to do. If he worked hard and fast enough, he might finish and be able to begin his math homework (Set 40), which he knew would be mentioned at the end of the period. He understood well this use of time before the beginning of the next lesson in reading.

Because he was in the second group in reading and because the planning of the teacher was well known to him (even though there was no open sharing of plans), he knew

that he would have to answer questions taken from the story he had read the day before. This was the way the teacher always did it. And he didn't mind.

The day proceeded in the usual fashion: getting out books, doing assignments, putting books back in the desk, being occupied with tasks, sitting in his chair, doing what was expected. From time to time, he glanced at Larry and Tommy next to him and whispered to them whenever he could without being detected. He made a funny face at one of his pals across the room. He even pinched one of the girls he liked while they were getting in line to go to the library.

All of this and more was Johnny's day. He understood it well. As he ran out of the building at 3:15 that afternoon, released from the requirements and expectations of the school day, he hurried to find his buddies and to get on to the ball game. He wanted to try out that new glove.

THE PRACTICE

Omissions for Johnny

Although each detail is not listed here, this description represents a fair sampling of Johnny's typical school day. Two notable elements are missing, however. For that matter, they are missing from most of Johnny's school days: individual contact and personalized relationship with the teacher.

Johnny's experience is not so different from that of the majority. Most students know school as a matter of following set patterns and procedure.

Quite a few students, however, fail to master the routines, regulations and rituals that Johnny knows so well. For the not-so-good Johnnies, individual contact is established, but only because they are misbehaving or hesitating to do an assignment. In either case it is rare for Johnny, good or bad, to know the teacher in a personal, human way. Indeed, students come to school, attend classrooms, work in spatial proximity of a few feet from the teacher and never experi-

4

ence a touch on the shoulder, a warm, direct look, or a verbal expression of encouragement. This lack of contact has far-reaching consequences. The student neither identifies with the teacher nor sees his own cause in being in school. As just one symptom of impersonal contact, it is clear that visual rejection of the presence of students can lead to dehumanization, alienation and withdrawal. But far more important than individual contact is the teacher's concern for educating the individual and being involved in his personal growth.

More has probably been written and spoken on the need to educate the individual, to humanize the person, and to focus on individual growth than perhaps on any other contemporary educational subject. But the results are few. More innovative ideas on individualized instruction were introduced in the fifties and sixties than in all of the years past; yet, the question of personalized instruction remains unanswered.

It was thought that the difficulty was easy to identify: organizational arrangements had merely not been flexible enough. The tricks were to change the self-contained classroom to departmentalized programs, to non-grade the school, to team-teach, to program instruction, and to individualize instruction. Changing the structure of schooling was considered the key, and it was thought that individualized learning could be assured. The lesson is all too clear: organizational changes do not ensure individual approaches to learning. What was considered to be one of the poorest arrangements for learning—the one-room school house—is now respected and revered because it is still assumed that organizational arrangements assure individual contact and learning. The best or the so-called worst organizational condition neither permits nor prevents our quest to educate the individual in his own direction.

In any organizational scheme, in any effort to educate the young, the willingness or ability of the teacher to relate individually to the student is essential. Contacts and displays of interest toward the student exact toil and demand much energy. For many teachers, it is easier to think of students collectively, of the class as a unified individual.

After all, "Teachers cannot be everywhere at once"; "It is impossible to teach thirty or more students in an individualized manner"; "Taking the time to relate to one student makes it possible for student misbehavior to occur elsewhere." To the teacher who truly wants to individualize teaching, such fears and rationalization are sheer nonsense.

The Teacher's Trap

It is not that teachers fail to understand the importance of teaching. Teachers know a great deal about teaching strategies. They know how to plan lessons well, to present information with clarity, to introduce ideas effectively, to summarize and achieve closure with concepts, to teach for behavioral objectives, to ask meaningful questions and, in the main, to control *their* teaching behaviors. These are important matters but they entrap teachers. Becoming preoccupied with the eloquence of their own performance rather than their response to students is the trap.

For teachers are usually far more eager to follow their own leads rather than student direction. For instance, how much thought and consideration has been given to the appropriate responses that might be made to the different kinds of questions students ask? How important is it to listen carefully when a student talks and to indicate an interest? How much time is spent determining a student's interest and proclivity in achieving a behavioral objective? In effect, we need to know much more about the student cause in learning and in following his leads to increased knowledge and experience.

6

In personalizing instruction it is receptivity and responsiveness that matter. The teacher neither waits nor sits idly by for a student to act but stands ready and alert to the direction and pace of student learning, which occurs through observation, analysis and responsiveness to student behavior. Being a teacher requires creative behaviors that come from sensitive and acute awareness. Specifically, the teacher listens more and the student talks more. He accepts the student as partner in deciding the value of behavioral goals. He wants to understand the energies and motivations of his students and analyzes them more carefully. He spends more time with individual students.

The teacher should be both able and willing to respond to student cause and direction in learning. Following the leads and directions of the learner in educating himself represents a more direct approach to personalized instruction and to individualized learning.

THE THEORY

The promise of "meeting the needs of the individual" can be more than a cliché; the basic organizing construct of the school can be a one-to-one relationship. Staff, resources, space, time and effort can all be organized so that the instructional effort can be tailored to fit the learning needs of each individual child. And money is not the most important problem. Basic assumptions are.

Theoretically, the taproots of educational programs draw their strength directly from what we know about the nature of (1) the individual (his abilities, motivations, development, and perceptual style) ; (2) the disciplines (the basic facts, concepts, methodology, and structure) ; (3) society (its cultural norms, institutional bases, language patterns, and population mobility). All three sources are important and theoretically could be put into operation equally and mutually as a base for educational assumptions. But, inevitably, curriculum builders tend to draw upon one of them as primary. If what we know about the nature of the disciplines is primary, some kind of subject-matter centered program, generally departmentalized, appears. Placing our knowledge about the nature of the individual as primary obviously generates yet another kind of educational program.

In the traditional elementary school, on the one hand, many proponents of the self-contained classroom advocate child-centered approaches and developmental notions, but in actual practice the child is not as important as the group. On the other hand, advocates of the non-graded school and team teaching start with specialized knowledge from the disciplines and organize the programmatic effort from a subject-matter centered base. Advocating one approach over another is pointless. The best of each must be retained but the weaknesses must be eliminated. A shift to a person-centered approach might be more appropriate.

New evidence underscores this need. Studies in recent years comparing the effectiveness of the "new mathematics" with that of the "old mathematics," or of the "new method" of teaching foreign language or concept development or reading with the old methods, usually produced a "no significant difference" result.

The least obvious but most powerful explanation for this phenomenon is simply that individuals differ. Everybody knows this, but our search for programs presumes otherwise. Yet no *programs* meet the individual needs of each child. Programs are *group* solutions to what are obviously *personal* learning needs.

Some youngsters learn rapidly, others slowly. Some children learn best when subject matter is sequenced so that "discovery" and the inductive type of thought are fostered; others when ideas are deductively and didactically presented. Some youngsters learn best when they experience things directly and concretely. Others learn best vicariously, when they are told. Some children learn better when their effort is spaced evenly for short periods over an extended period of time, others when they are impressed completely and wholly in an experience for a concentrated period of time.

8

No one content or method or organizational concept or teaching style suits every individual child. Children differ. Because they do, instructional strategies, organizational arrangements, sequencing of knowledge and curriculum content must vary too. *What teachers do must occur as a function of the individual learner's learning needs.* Teacher behavior and curriculum content and organizational schemes must be *varied* because they are "variables" which must be manipulated to meet the *constant* of a given youngster's learning needs.

THE MODEL

What teachers do should follow from and be a function of what children do, not the other way around. The methods they employ, the curriculum content they select and the organizational framework within which they operate must be determined *after* observations of individual children's learning needs, not before. Teachers must make precise observations of particular, unique persons before they decide what they intend to do. "Group norms," "grade level" expectations and descriptions of "typical children" cannot be applied to this important task. School organization must facilitate learning for each individual child in the same way. Organizational arrangements should not be continued indeterminably because teachers prefer them or administrators like them or experts advocate them or publishers prefer them. Schools exist to help young people learn. The organizational aspects of the school must guarantee personalized instruction for every individual child.

Two assumptions are paramount in this respect: (1) what we know and can learn about the nature of the individual must be the primary source of curriculum (and what we know about the nature of society and the nature of knowledge must be secondary), and (2) the basic organizing construct of the school must be a one-to-one relationship between teacher and child. Especially important are matters that involve deployment of staff, employment of time, organization and segmentation of subject matter, and evaluation concepts and procedures.

Diversified Responsibilities

First, in a school organized to assure personalized instruction and individualized learning, professional personnel would be differentiated in both function and responsibility. In a typical elementary school, for example, there might be five master teachers, each having primary responsibility for 150 youngsters' learning. These children would range in age from six to thirteen (all grade levels). Master teachers would be highly competent, general practitioners of teaching, with doctors' degrees and extensive training in all subject matter fields and with children of all ages. Their salary should be about two and one-half times the average teacher's salary today. They would spend about 85 percent of their time with children in a one-to-one relationship, and about 15 percent coordinating and supervising activities of a staff performing highly specialized tasks under their supervision.

A typical eight-hour day (with no homework papers to correct or lesson plans to make, the school day would be extended) might be so arranged that four hours would be devoted to individual children on a 20-minute, one-to-one basis, with children visiting the master teacher according to a planned schedule. One hour and a half might be devoted to supervisory and coordinating activities with the specialists in the school. Two hours and a half could be available for additional 20- or 30-minute sessions with individual children on an "unscheduled" basis.

By using themselves in highly "focused" ways with individual children, master teachers would *first observe* and *then respond* with specific suggestions and instructions. These would be based upon their intimate interaction with and knowledge of each child. For example, they would observe student behavior in a clinical way (in a one-to-one setting, watching overt behaviors, studying particular test scores, listening to speech articulations, noting manifesta-

10

tions of anxiety, developing and studying case histories, watching muscular movements during writings), and they would guide learning activities with students for subsequent specialized purposes (listening to *this* lecture, reading *that* book, participation in *this* discussion group for three days, building such-and-such a model, visiting a given plant manager who employs a particular human relations technique with his staff). They would use dictaphones and other devices to maintain a continuous and comprehensive record of contact with each child, and these records would be available before and during each one-to-one interaction. Such teachers would not be givers of information, record keepers, scorers of tests or graders of homework. They would be extremely sensitive and highly trained general practitioners of teaching with in-depth knowledge of the basic disciplines, learning, motivation, personality structure, measurement, and the fundamental learning skills.

Four groups of specialists would work under the five master teachers' direction and supervision. One group might include six persons especially competent in the areas of reading and the language arts. Two of these might be highly proficient in developmental reading and literature, two in diagnostic and remedial reading, and two in expressive communicative skills (writing, speaking, spelling).

Another group might include two persons trained in mathematics and the natural sciences, two in mathematics and the physical sciences, one registered nurse who might teach health and safety as well as serve as the school nurse, and one person trained in physical education.

A third group might include eight persons with a particular competency in various areas of the creative arts and humanities. Two of these might have extensive training in music, two in art, and four in social studies and group processes.

A fourth team of four persons might consist of one counseling or clinical evaluator, one psychometrician, and two instructional materials center specialists. These specialists should probably receive about the same salary as a fifth-year teacher receives today.

The master teachers and the various specialists would require about ten secretaries (one to work for each of the master teachers, one for each of the four groups of specialists and one for the principal) and about twenty homeroom managers who would provide the continuity, "Homebase," and basic record cumulation files. Homeroom managers should be especially warm, accepting, and nurturant persons but not necessarily trained beyond clerical level. These paraprofessionals should probably receive approximately one-half the salary a regular teacher receives today.

To have educators working with children of three different levels of professional competency (i.e., master teachers, specialist teachers, and paraprofessionals) would mean that at any given time the 750 children might be deliberately dispersed this way among the various staff members: 5 children with the five master teachers; 18 children with the six reading, language art specialists; 12 children with the four math-science specialists; 8 children for a nurse-health educator; 20 children with the physical educator; 40 children with the two music educators; 20 children with the two art educators; 40 children with four social studies educators; one child with one counseling evaluator; one child with one psychometrist, 570 children with twenty homeroom managers; and 20 children with two instructional materials specialists.

In a typical school with 750 children, principals presently make $12,000, teachers approximately $8,000, secretaries approximately $4,000 and additional personnel available to the school from central office or on a relating basis make approximately $8,000. This is a total of approximately $300,000 annually for salaries.

In the proposed outline here, if a principal made $12,000, master teachers made $20,000, specialist teachers made $8,000, secretaries made $4,000, and homeroom managers made $3,000, the cost in instructional salaries for the year would be about $400,000.

Time Variations

Second, professional personnel would be differentiated in employment of time. If master teachers spend six and one-half hours every day with individual children on a one-to-one basis, these hours during the course of a year would amount to approximately 1170. Seeing each child about 20 minutes each session would mean approximately 3500 one-to-one sessions during a 180-day school year. Working with a basic group of 150 youngsters, each master would have between 20 and 25 one-to-one sessions of 20 minutes each with every one of his 150 children during the course of the school year. Specialists would work with children in groups of three to ten and for periods of time running from 20 to 90 minutes so that teacher-pupil interaction could be highly personalized. Since no child would ever be in a group of more than 30, and almost a third of his time would be spent in groups of less than ten, his opportunity to interact with teachers at a highly personal level would be greatly enhanced.

Making Subject Matter Usable

Third, with a school organized so that the development of the individual learner is primary, subject matter becomes a means to that end. The conventional concerns regarding subject matter content (continuity, scope, sequence, articulation, etc.) are much less important than using "pieces" of knowledge to fit and form the logic of a growing learner's mind. Content would be segmented and organized to make many small "pieces" readily available to the specialists (working closely with the master teacher), to build curriculum within each student. Focusing sharply upon the basic domain of each discipline (generalizations, facts, concepts, assumptions) and the techniques and procedures unique to the various subject matter fields, subject matter could be organized and categorized for "storage" and recall with maximum effectiveness and minimum time. "Pieces" would be small and of such a nature that they would require one minute to three days to be utilized by the learner. Literally thousands of individual units would be available to the master teacher and the specialists, and there would be no such things as "textbook adoption" for all children, "uniform" materials or standards, "school-wide" examinations, "grade level" subjects, "textbook series" for grades one through three, or the like.

The number of "combinations" of curriculum pieces will be large, so that the potential for "creating" curriculum for each child will be very great. Because the "pieces" can be combined and recombined in almost an infinite number of ways, experimentation with facts and concepts will be both essential and continuous. Both the learner and the teacher will experience the thrill of continuously discovering new patterns of meaning and knowledge as they use information to form and foster growth.

Changes in Evaluation Techniques

Fourth, in dealing with evaluation concepts and procedures, less concern for statistical reliability and more with validity will be evident. Schoolmen will move away from tests that are verbal, timed, multiple choice, and pencil-and-paper toward developing instruments and techniques on assessing individual accomplishment and growth. Master teachers, especially, will be trained as clinicians—competent *subjective* evaluators who use themselves as an evaluating tool in assessing motivation, learning style, achievement and learning. *Objective* procedures would be extensive and elaborate, but they would typically be non-verbal, non-timed, non-normed instruments to produce raw score data which professional teachers could use to make inferences about children's intellectual and emotional growth.

JOHNNY REVISITED

As Johnny walked toward the entrance of his school, he met a couple of friends on the way in. They stopped to talk about the ball game they were going to play in the afternoon and then entered the multiclassed building.

Johnny went directly to the library, took a seat, and began to work on his independent project. After opening school

YOUR
IDEAS
ARE
GREAT!

exercises, he continued to gather information from the sources he found. If he worked hard and fast enough, he might have more to say to the teacher when they discussed his ideas, which he knew would be the purpose of their getting together. This use of time on his own before he met with one of his teachers was something he understood well.

Because he was doing his own project and because the activities of his teachers were well known to him (because there was an open sharing of plans), he knew that he would have to get to work, for there were many other things to look forward to this day. And the focus was usually on his own interests and achievements. This was the way the teachers always seemed to put it. And he liked it that way.

The day proceeded in the usual fashion: using books, doing his own assignments, putting the materials back in their designated places, being occupied with tasks, sitting in many chairs, participating in the continuing seminar, doing what he expected. From time to time, he looked at Larry and Tommy next to him, and talked to them about his work whenever he could. He made a funny face at one of his pals across the room. He even pinched one of the girls he liked while they were getting in line at the cafeteria.

All of this and more was Johnny's day. He understood it well. As he left the building at 4:00 that afternoon, released from the hard work and free time of the school day, he hurried to find his buddies and to get on to the ball game without delay. He wanted to try out that new glove.

The changing role
of the teacher

Vito Perrone
New School of Behavioral Studies
The University of North Dakota

2

A discussion of the changing role of the teacher presupposes organic changes in our schools. Although many people still argue that our schools are functioning well and do not need to change, objective evidence is quite to the contrary. In 1951 Margaret Mead reported:

> American children are growing up within the most rapidly changing culture of which we have any record in the world, within a culture where for several generations each generation's experience has differed sharply from the last, and in which the experience of the youngest child in a large family will be extraordinarily different from that of the first born. Mothers can not look to the experience of their mothers, nor even to that of their older sisters; young husbands and fathers have no guides to the behavior which they are assuming today. So long standing and so rapid have been those processes

of change that expectation of change and anxiety about change have been built into our character as a people.[1]

Eighteen years later in an address on "Youth Today" Margaret Mead went even further in describing change:

> The difference between the lives of the pre-World War II generations and today's youth is as great as the span between the oldsters and the savages of New Guinea. . . . (Teachers and parents cannot look to their own experiences to understand youth.) It is as if one group is speaking Japanese and one is speaking English and they are under the illusion they are talking the same language.[2]

The historian, Carl Bridenbaugh, put it a little differently, but his point was similar:

> The nature of human existence has undergone a great mutation. . . . So pervading and complete has been this change, and so complex has life become . . . that it now appears probable that mid-nineteenth century America or Western Europe had more in common with fifth-century Greece (physically, economically, socially, mentally, spiritually) than with their own projections into the middle of the twentieth century.[3]

Marshall McLuhan and George Leonard recently stated that "schooling as we now know it may be only a memory. . . . Fragmentation, specialization, and sameness will be replaced by wholeness, diversity, and above all, a deep involvement . . . schools will be more concerned with training the senses and perceptions than with stuffing brains." [4]

---

1. "The Impact of Culture on Personality Development in the United States Today," *Understanding the Child* 20 (January 1951): 17-181.

2. *Education U.S.A.*, National School Public Relations Association, NEA, March 3, 1969, p. 147.

3. "The Great Mutation," *American Historical Review 68* (January 1963): 316-17.

4. "The Future of Education: The Class of 1989," *Look* (February 21, 1967): 23-25. Reprinted by permission of Harold Ober Associates, Incorporated. Copyright © 1967 by Cowles Communications Incorporated.

John I. Goodlad has suggested that "today's schools are obsolescent . . . designed for a different culture, a different conception of learning and teaching, and a different clientele." [5]

Our rhetoric has long expressed the need for enhancing individuality, fostering creativity, and assisting children to become independent learners. Mere rhetoric is not enough. The time has come to create valid psychological and physical environments that promote those ends. Such environments —free and always changing—should reflect contemporary society and of necessity contribute to the changing role of the teacher.

A CHANGING ENVIRONMENT

A summary description of classrooms that promote individuality in learning seems appropriate before discussing the resultant demands made upon a teacher. Central to the philosophy behind such classrooms is the provision for a variety of learning environments in school and out. A number of interest centers in different content and subject areas provide a setting for children to develop their skills, understandings and appreciations. A multiplicity of curriculum materials, tools, and other stimuli, which children can produce themselves, are essential in the interest centers. Children are free to engage in different activities, working both independently and in small groups. Learning progresses at a rate appropriate to each child's capacities, interests, and needs rather than at a rate prescribed by teacher, curriculum, or graded groupings. Choices for children are broad, creating many opportunities for success experiences that nurture a positive self-concept. Concern for the quality of interpersonal relationships validates ungraded organizational patterns. When properly handled, it permits older children to help younger, brighter to assist less bright;

---

5. "The Future of Teachers and Learning," Washington: NEA, Occasional Paper, 1968, p. 4.

it also encourages development of appropriate self-discipline without undue reliance upon the authority of the teacher. The lines between subject areas such as science, social studies, language arts and mathematics are allowed to mesh.

And what does all this mean for the teacher? This concern certainly means a more rewarding relationship with children and learning; it also means an enormous physical and intellectual effort. Sybil Marshall, in a "note to the young teacher" suggested:

> To control a class in freedom, to learn with each child instead of instructing a passive class, to be a well of clear water into which the children can dip all the time, instead of a hosepipe dousing them with facts, is the most exhausting way of all of doing a teacher's job.[6]

New teaching skills and attitudes are necessary as teachers move from a role of imparter of information and occupant of the center stage to that of an observer, stimulator, guide and assistant to each of the children, manager of time, space, and materials, and student of learner behavior.

INCREASED UNDERSTANDING ESSENTIAL

The teacher needs an increased understanding of the processes of learning and their implications for teaching. It is clear that much of our present practice in schools is contrary to what is known about learning. The typical teacher is not at present well prepared to handle this "changing" classroom. Desiring to help children, she yet may be weak in diagnostic skills, out-of-touch with the literature in her fields, and limited in her knowledge of children.

An increased understanding of the learning process is essential to the diagnostic role of the teacher in the individualized, open classroom. Recognizing that children learn at different rates and have differing self-concepts and learn-

---

6. *An Experiment in Education* (Cambridge: Cambridge University Press, 1966), p. 42.

ing styles leads to the use of diverse learning materials and approaches for each child. In stressing the individualized classroom environment, I do not mean to imply that every teacher who moves in that direction possesses a greater understanding of the learning process. I have seen many individualized classrooms that are little more than supervised "correspondence schools," where personal interaction is slight, where "paper-and-pencil" activities predominate. The kinds of understanding teachers need to affirm would preclude reliance on such limited approaches to learning in a classroom.

Diagnosis demands that records be kept on each child, noting where the child is, what he has accomplished, what learnings he has achieved. Such record keeping is necessary in a setting where children are working with various materials at different rates, where curriculum is not absolutely fixed, and learning experiences are relatively unstructured. Part of the diagnostic function essential to providing for individual needs, record keeping clearly calls for an *increased intensity of involvement* with individual children.

Enhancing individuality in learning also demands more cooperative, less threatening relationships among its members, children and teachers alike. The teacher must remove himself from a purely judgmental role in the classroom in order to maximize the intrinsic interest in learning that children bring with them to school. The teacher needs to assist children to learn for themselves rather than from fear of rejection or desire for praise. The affective psychological climate should be more central to teachers' concerns. This takes a new preparation, and experience suggests that it is a difficult preparation inasmuch as it calls for a change in a teacher's basic orientation toward teaching.

FREEDOM TO BE FLEXIBLE

Teachers have long relied on someone else's textbooks, teachers' manuals, curriculum guides and the like to provide a formal classroom structure. The individualized, open class-

room, however, places a larger degree of responsibility for the design as well as the implementation of learning squarely on the shoulders of the teacher or teachers. Curriculum control must be centered primarily in the classroom if individualization is to have much meaning.

To function at a maximum level, teachers cannot be so confined by traditional courses of study, textbooks, examinations and administrators that they are unable to participate in the creative task of guiding the learning process of individual children. Time schedules, and the security that has accompanied them, can no longer be so rigid. Flexibility must prevail; and contrary to what many teachers and laymen seem to believe, that flexibility demands more planning. It might take months to plan new experiences. The planning and the necessary evaluation of ongoing experiences produce more tension in teachers than any other facet of their work. The demands on teachers are, of necessity, increasing.

For individualized classrooms, where most learning decisions are made by teachers and students, selection of a variety of materials and learning situations become even more

21

important. The teacher, in this ever-changing setting, must be equipped to select materials from an ever-growing reservoir that includes "packaged" materials, television, radio, film, audiotape and computers. He needs to be better grounded in what materials to look for and how they can meet the needs of individual children. Because of the vast material resources available, the teacher needs to develop a greater understanding of the relationships between learning and the learning materials.

DIVERSITY IN MATERIALS

An important thing to stress in the use of diverse materials is that they need not all be commercial. Some of the best materials are those developed by teachers and children themselves from common components to be found in the community. In a small North Dakota community, a teacher and a class of eight- to nine-year-olds turned a discarded bathtub into an extraordinary aquarium. The variety of water life grows by the week. Putting the old tub to such good use has caught the interest of the community and has led to learning experiences not only in science but also in art, mathematics and language arts.

Using common materials can serve another useful purpose, that of assisting in the development of more stimulating home environments for children. Parents visiting a classroom and viewing vast stores of expensive commercial equipment must resign themselves to being able to contribute little to a significant learning environment in the home. And children will be less likely to involve themselves in really creative enterprises at home, which may grow out of, or grow into, experiences at school.

To develop individualized, open classrooms, a school should bring together diverse talents and experiment with differentiated staffing patterns. We know that increasing the ratio of productive, sensitive adults to children in classrooms has positive results. Team teaching (or cooperative teaching) and increased use of teacher assistants (or teacher aides) provide children with a wider variety of learning experiences, representing increased opportunity for meeting individual needs.

COOPERATIVE TEACHING

Cooperative teaching provides a wider outlet for a teacher with a particular enthusiasm for an area of learning. Children recognize, especially in a program that capitalizes on the interests they promote, that teachers have limitations. And teachers surely are aware of their own strengths and weaknesses. Cooperative teaching relationships provide important outlets for children and teachers to seek assistance. It is an important mechanism for stimulating the professional growth of the teachers involved. Cooperative teaching relationships also provide a positive environment into which part-time, community resource teachers can easily fit.

The increased use of teacher aides has provided professional teachers with more time for instructional tasks. Housekeeping, clerical tasks, and routine assistance to children occupy the greater part of most teachers' time. This is wasteful. Although many teachers find satisfaction in such routine activities, their professional role is more significant. Teacher aides can help with routine work. Debate still continues about the extent of a teacher aide's duties, especially as it relates to face-to-face instructional type relationships with children; yet we must not waste human resources. There cannot be too much assistance by aides in the kind of classroom under discussion here. A classroom with additional adult staff does, however, pose new problems for teachers. Openness is necessary. Learning to plan with others, including children, is a new demand on teachers who, in most instances, are not experienced in small group interaction.

Coupled with differentiated staffing patterns is a revival of multi-age groupings, a natural pattern that removes much of the pressure that teachers face at the end of a school year as they panic about whether "Johnny" knows enough mathematics or spelling. After all, what will "Miss Brown," the teacher in the next grade level, think? Multi-age patterns permit the teacher to have at least two years to work with children at their own pace, and continuity frees the teacher considerably in her expectation levels; what to do if a child isn't reading by age six becomes less crucial. Multi-age grouping puts vividly before teachers the fact that they are dealing with children that are not all alike.

The kind of involvement that is desired calls for greater ties to the immediate school community. Teachers need to be far more aware of the many-dimensioned world outside the classroom and its influences on children. Increased involvement with parents is desirable. Rather than talk to parents, which has been the traditional pattern, teachers need to talk *with* parents. Again, this is a new and important demand on teachers.

Basic to much of the foregoing is a trust in children. One might argue that teachers have always trusted children, but evidence of such trust is lacking. An environment that fosters individuality cannot function at an optimal level unless the teacher respects learners as persons and trusts that children can learn and want to learn. It demands a teacher who is secure and is always learning.

Universities and colleges have for too long been too far removed from elementary schools. If teacher-training institutions are to be successful in preparing teachers for their new classroom roles as participants in more active learning environments, much more of the preparation will have to take place in actual classrooms. This affords the pre-service teacher an opportunity to investigate in a very concrete way the general hypotheses that have grown out of his study. It also affords him the opportunity to refine his skills and insights into the nature of learning and to reinforce his commitments. Such use of the classroom for preparation of teachers suggests that the teacher in the classroom, especially the individualized open classroom, must also become a teacher-trainer. The role of teacher-trainer is an important one that must go far beyond the traditional apprentice-supervisor type situations that have been common with student teaching experiences.

In the changing American educational scene teachers must become prepared to meet the new demands of their changing role. Otherwise schools will remain uninteresting and become increasingly irrelevant to the lives of children. And teachers will not realize the full satisfaction their profession should provide.

Organization for individual work

David E. Day and *Dwight W. Allen*
School of Education, The University of Massachusetts

3

Innovations regarding organization for instruction, the roles of teachers and other school personnel, and the kinds of instructional materials must be interpreted on the basis of what we continue to discover about the nature of the human organism. So it is, too, with the kinds of provisions that are made for individual work. Through implications arising from, among other things, our growing knowledge of human behavior, we have learned that:

1. The early years—birth to age seven or eight—are a period of very rapid growth. Bloom (1) has even suggested that this is the time of greatest psychosocial, physical, and intellectual growth and development. It would appear that what takes place in schools—in any school—at this time should not only contribute to the acceleration of growth but should capitalize on it as well.

2. It has been demonstrated in many ways that growth is modifiable. What each of us becomes is a response to the

mix and interaction of both genetic and experiential or environmental factors. A child, regardless of inherited limits, may not develop the ability to sit up or to use language as the prime means of communication unless conditions in his environment demand such behaviors.

3. Although periods of life are characterized by more or less rapid growth, individual growth is idiosyncratic. There is every reason to believe that six-year-old children can learn to read; most of them do with ease. This bit of knowledge should not, however, be interpreted as a rationale for teaching all children six years of age reading at the same time or in the same way. A seven-year-old may in some ways be more like an eleven-year-old child than like other children his age. A nine-year-old might exhibit some behavior commonly associated with infancy. In spite of this knowledge, we persist in asking the wrong kinds of questions: i.e., what is the best way of grouping seven-year-olds?

4. Our work in discovering the ways in which children learn is primitive but our knowledge of the existence of different styles of learning seems well established. Irving Sigel (2), for example, has demonstrated differences in the ways by which children organize and group objects, thereby hypothesizing about the nature of the intellectual activity taking place. Others now tell us that some children can gather data better through one sense than another and that the situation may determine the effectiveness of the senses.

5. For convenience' sake we speak of psychosocial, physical and intellectual development of the human organism. We are convinced of the interrelationship and reject any dualistic or separatism conceptions. Clearly, curricula are developed, emphases are determined, and myths are created on the basis of this compartmentalization of the human being. We have adhered to a belief that if intellectual development is emphasized in the education of young children, then the psyche will be damaged. There is no evidence supporting the contention that emphasis on intellectual development

of young children negatively affects their psychosocial development (3).

There are other general statements one could make. These seem most important in considering the process of organization for individual school work of young children. Immediate implications of these statements would include the following:

Multiple Person Contact. A prime factor in considering ways of effecting improved organization for individual work is increased intimate student-to-other contact. Provision must be made for students to work with other students—older and younger—as team learners. Students must have increased and regular interaction with adults. Our young children must also be given increased opportunity to work as a teacher with other children. It seems possible that these goals can be realized with the resources available in the schools, but not presently being used. A not uncommon sight in schools today is that of two or three children aged 10 or older working together on a science or math problem. Many materials designed to produce either observable behaviors or conceptual systems, or both, rely heavily on student-to-student participation in assisting one another. The model seems sound; the practice needs to be used with young children.

A child's language maturity, ability to reason logically, and social response to another child in a situation requiring mutual respect can be developed even when playing checkers. A child who knows how to play the game can teach others, and what does this require of verbal skills? A child who understands the concept of sets being groups of like items can teach this to another with perhaps greater skill than his teacher. Why shouldn't a child having great difficulty understanding relative size and distance actively solicit help from his peers? Furthermore, shouldn't the school work hard at creating a climate that fosters this kind of person-to-person interaction? Clearly this is not an attitude fostered in most schools we have visited, but it could be.

Massachusetts has recently recognized the importance of early education, and legislation passed in 1968 now requires universal public kindergarten by 1973. The legislators' wisdom in this matter was long overdue. The actions to date, however, show a failure to comprehend the importance of close, intimate adult contact in the early years of education. The legislators have recommended a teacher-pupil ratio of 1 to 25 with each teacher meeting two groups of children each day, but in fact the ratio becomes 1 to 50. Given our knowledge of what must be done in kindergarten if it is to become a real arm of education, these suggestions become ludicrous. The situation can be salvaged, however, if we accept and adopt another new and important education concept: differentiated staffing.

For too long we have assumed that the only adult capable of working with a child in the school was the fully certificated teacher. One could hypothesize about the degree to which federal funds for school aides and paraprofessionals contributed to our changing view on this matter. We have

brought adults into the school, but we have not yet begun to employ them in much save custodial or clerical activities.

We can and should think of using parents as aides, teaching interns, fully trained teaching assistants, and as beginning-level teachers with persons of greater skill in the teaching process. We can increase student-adult contact without increasing instructional personnel costs if we agree that (1) adults other than teachers can teach children; (2) beginning teachers are not fully trained and need supervision and direction; (3) the responsibility for program development and instructional design can be allocated to a highly skilled supervising teacher. A differentiated staffing program as outlined by Allen (4) could increase markedly the chances for high quality kindergarten education in Massachusetts if it were implemented.

Exploration Without Sanctions. Reflect for a moment on the five general statements about development. Implicit in all that is said is that the child, at whatever age, needs an opportunity to explore all manner of events without the imposition of sanctions for straying. Individual work includes diversion. A child must be assured that if he chooses to follow an interest, a lead, or a fellow student simply because he is interested, this kind of behavior will be accepted.

Whenever a student follows his own lead he must be called upon to reflect on it. Operationalized, this would be asking a child to tell you all he could about his attempt to build a tower out of triangle- and diamond-shaped blocks, or what he might have discovered from watching hornets build a nest in an outside corner of a window. The point of emphasis is on the student's perception and not on a pre-established set of goals. The teaching paradigm is success rather than fail-success so often used today. Whatever a child relates after an idiosyncratic exploration is accepted. He learns that he can generate knowledge and that whatever is generated is not at the moment subjected to the test of acceptability. Our impression is that teachers are still a long way from operating on this distinction.

Perhaps the most valuable and important factor in being able to explore freely is that it probably will result in syntheses of separate and unknowingly related phenomena. As the child grows, he struggles constantly with problems of organizing stimuli and attributes of those stimuli. He experiments with language as a vehicle in testing interrelationships. We are fairly well convinced at this point that we have different kinds and types of systems for organizing different phenomena and *that it takes time for all of us to complete the organization.* A child may "know" that it takes water, heat, and light to maintain plant and animal life, but he may never "discover" the relationship of plant to animal life—and that too much or too little water, heat, and light as well as plant or animal life will destroy the balance of life for all—until he examines the remains of a sunbaked terrarium and remembers what had happened to the bean seeds soaked with water each day.

The point itself should be clear. Individual work means individual time—for exploration and synthesis—in a situation that rewards rather than punishes this kind of behavior.

Intellectually Demanding Activities. Exploration without sanctions creates an attitude that searching is valuable, and this is good. Unfortunately, for teachers and children, the exploring behavior by itself is not enough; care must be taken to provide means by which the mind of the child can be stretched. This implies that organizational decision must take into account provisions for increasingly more complex and demanding activities. The concepts of sequence and hierarchy become extremely important here.

Although we can't agree on the pattern of development, it is clear that intellectual development takes place in stages or levels. A child is not born with the same intellectual skills he will have at age six or twelve or as an adult. It is clear too, that these skills can be affected—positively and negatively—by the kinds of stimuli the child experiences. The assumption that full potential (full growth) can be achieved if the organism is left alone has been demonstrated to be mythology by, among other things, the research on sensory deprivation. Deutsch (5) has suggested that a difference between an advantaged and disadvantaged learner is to be found in the kinds of responses required of the child to more than random stimuli. The advantaged learner is asked by parents and peers to explain, to demonstrate, to copy, to listen to and to follow directions carefully. Further, the nature of controlled stimuli increases over time. The quality of stimuli and the intensity with which it is given seem to be a natural function of growing up in an advantaged family. Unfortunately, one can often examine post facto the experience of children who have difficulty handling complex situations and discover that they were neither required to engage in differential examination of their environment nor was the environment controlled with the intent of increasing verbal and other intellectual skills.

Organization for individual work has as a prime goal the full development of every child. Special care must be taken to ensure the intellective growth is not affected adversely in the name of meeting interests and needs.

Much is being said today about the need to increase the emphasis on cognitive development in elementary schools, particularly with the very young. As much is heard decrying this move and suggesting that the school has emphasized cognitive skills out of proportion to affective development. A word needs to be said lest one think that what has been suggested plays into the hands of any who could defend or refute this contention.

The schools have not yet really begun to tap the potential for intellectual development. Emphasis on subject matter is just that. It is not emphasis on child development. The question of whether or not a child of eight should be taught French or German is a question of the purpose of education and not a matter of the way in which a child will come to know. Furthermore, emphasis on teaching youngsters predetermined conceptual systems must clearly be understood as an emphasis on both curriculum content and the bias of those scholars who built the curriculum. One is hard pressed to find any relationship between what we have described as intellectual development and most of what we see in the modern curriculum movement. It is not a question of the school not really considering cognitive growth; the schools are pushing new packages of already predetermined knowledge. How can this be confused with the struggle of the human organism to know his world and to achieve order in it?

Provisions for Self Evaluation. Whether we talk about elaborate systems with feedback loops or programmed instructional devices with which a child works alone or with one or two peers, ways must be available for him to determine his progress toward a clearly defined goal. In fact, when we organize for individual work, we must: (1) make sure the objectives are clearly specified and understood by the child; (2) arrange the learning situation so that the learner can see both the beginning and the end, and whatever alternative routes are designed to get him where he is going; and (3) make it possible for the child to judge to what degree he is accomplishing his objectives at any time. In short, *the question of progress or of judging how well he is doing should be made by the child,* and the instructional system must take this into account.

We often ask children to observe phenomena and to make judgments on their observations. This happens when a five-year-old is asked to name the objects in an urban scene that are green, for example, or when a twelve-year-old develops some researchable hypothesis about the effect of heat on metal. If a child is to be able to work independently on problems such as these, instructional schema must be designed that will tell the child immediately when he has made a correct and incorrect choice. There is no question that this will be a difficult task. It is often difficult, however, not impossible—as has been shown by Suppes' work with CAI and Lassar Gotkin's development of instructional games.

At times all of us become quite anxious when we are faced with propositions which, on the surface, appear to demand an incredible amount of structure. Those of us who expound the absolute necessity for defining educational objectives in behavioral terms have moments when we are unsure—when we wonder about the effects of carefully plotted goals on the perception and attitude of the child. So it is with what we've just said. Aren't we really contradicting what we said about exploration when we call for those provisions for evaluation by the student? Not so! What is being suggested is an instructional scheme that will make the greatest number of provisions for unique individual growth. Furthermore, exploration is a goal! Provisions for its happening must be judged on the basis of how well a child is encouraged to explore or on the basis of how many impediments are found. The problem arises when we fail to differentiate between the behaviors involved in reading, for example, and in relating all we can about a turtle. Both are as legitimate school behaviors as they are different. Each would require a different series of alternative instructional procedures but both should demand clarity of purpose and provision for evaluation of performance.

Greater Freedom of Movement. More than a decade ago Ole Sand implored us to look beyond the 2 x 4 school. Given what we know about the child and the range of interests and abilities any collection of thirty students would have, it seems axiomatic that we move beyond the four walls of a classroom and the two covers of a book in organizing for individual work. A child must have both the freedom to explore and access to a wealth of resources ranging far beyond those possible to include in the richest single classroom environment.

More and more schools are experimenting with the creation of a whole school as the locus of formal education rather than the classroom. In some places we find the library has become an instructional resources center where children are free to go for any manner of assistance. Other schools are being built without thirty-child classroom modules. Children are grouped loosely by any number of criteria other than age, grade, or achievement. Occasionally we hear of school districts that encourage teaching personnel to move away from the school for instructional purposes and to make formal arrangements to use artists, businessmen, and political leaders as instructors.

Unfortunately, we have few examples of what we've just described. Worse yet, Goodlad (6) has discovered much to his dismay that those ideas emphasized by Sand are for the most part still just ideas.

Change in education has been characterized by a lag of fifty years between idea and practice. Some could say the lag is not unreasonably severe. Others suggest it is scandalously long. The fact that ideas move slowly from page to practice must be examined not in terms of how the gap can be closed but rather in terms of possibility. Questions such as "Can it be done? Would it be economically feasible?" and "Would it improve instruction?" must be raised. If the answers to those queries are positive, then the matter of the lag becomes moot. The issue would be the apparent unwillingness of the profession to move in spite of evidence pointing out the advantages of doing so. One might postulate that the reason we see so little attention given to providing the greatest range of student instructional choices is that we in the profession have chosen not to do so.

There are other implications derived from what we know about the way a child grows and develops. It seems obvious that we must develop a system of continuous assessment of a child's growth, producing a constantly changing profile of growth that would be of both prescriptive and descriptive value. This is so because the concept of grade has long since outlived its usefulness.

Perhaps the major impetus for our considering the question of organization for individual instruction has come from the relatively new belief that the young child is intellectually alert and potentially very active. In addition, we seem to have demonstrated that his growth can be dulled and impaired by sedentary activities that provide little by way of demanding participation. Developing mathematical computation skills by drill, learning to read in "the group," or "having art class" will never be a positive factor in the development of most children. Organizing a school around such curriculum components as aesthetics, human relationships, language development, and inquiry where the major instructional unit is the individual could lead to the full development of individual potential—which is, after all, our major objective.

Our concern, too, is for creativity. It would seem that we need generations who will be able to lead us out of the seemingly unsolvable problems of present day life. We need persons who are able to leap beyond the bounds of traditional thought and solutions, and these types cannot be mass produced by sterile modal-organized school systems. A creative person is one who can see new relationships based on even keener perception. Perceptual awareness is not a birthright but a skill developed carefully and requiring considerable environmental support. The creative act consists of, among other things, *achieving clarity and order in the universe, whatever the dimensions.* School should be designed as a place where the individual can develop this behavior.

If one fully intends to design a classroom for individual work, he will soon come to understand that seatwork, workbooks, and contrived creative activities are really ways of controlling children's behavior while the teacher is busy at other tasks. If the teacher believes, as we do, that the child can be responsible for a considerable amount of his behavior and that instructional alternatives can be designed, then he will come to appreciate a workbook as a potentially valuable resource and seatwork as a choice. At any rate, we know that we as teachers have the choice.

REFERENCES

1. Bloom, Benjamin. *Stability and Change in Human Characteristics.* New York: John Wiley, 1964.
2. Sigel, Irving, and P. Almstead. *Styles of Categorization Among Lower-Class Kindergarten Children.* Paper presented at American Educational Research Association Annual Meeting, New York City, February 1967.
3. Fowler, William. "Cognitive Learning in Infancy and Early Childhood," *Psychological Bulletin* 59 (1962): 116-52.
4. Allen, Dwight. "A Differentiated Staff: Putting Teaching Talent to Work," *Occasional Papers*, National Commission on Teacher Education and Professional Standards, NEA, Washington, D.C. 1967.
5. Deutsch, Martin. "The Disadvantaged Child and the Learning Process: Some Social and Developmental Consideration," in A. Harry Passow, *Education in Depressed Areas*, New York: Bureau of Publication, Teachers College, Columbia University, 1963.
6. Goodlad, John I. "The Schools vs. Education," *Saturday Review*, April 19, 1969, p. 59.

Evaluating and recording children's activities: diagnosing educational need

Bill Elliott, Director Pupil Personnel Services
Goleta Union School District, California
Mary Jo Woodfin, Department of Education
California State College at Long Beach

4

Diagnosis ... unmet need ... individualized instruction ... continuous progress ... team planning. ... Excedrin headache #73!

DIAGNOSIS REDEFINED

Diagnosis is the villain. All the changes in organization, roles, and teaching strategies described in this bulletin follow from the identification and analysis of unmet student need. The surge of creative response to diagnosed need has acted reciprocally on our understanding of educational diagnosis. Now we know that diagnostic study must deal with the educational system itself (and all the people in it, including ourselves) as well as with the student. It is a complex task we educators now share.

Having just experienced in microcosm the nature of this complexity in preparing this article, we would like to share the experience as a model for our expanded definition of diagnosis.

The individual writer (a school psychologist) reviews the definition of need, makes his response in a first draft, but feels dissatisfied with his efforts. He needs curriculum help; he asks for it, and in asking becomes a member of a teaching team. "No longer alone! Together we can do the job!"

The team goes to work but soon becomes hung up, each angry at himself and teammate . . . no time to talk . . . must talk (diagnosis at team level). Out of the discussion comes better definition of the task, sharing of the experiences of team members which condition their responses to the task, development of team purpose and direction. Back to work.

The cycle repeats several times. Work . . . talk about objectives . . . work . . . evaluate, etc. As with most first team efforts, the product may be a bit lumpy, but we take some pride in it. Next time it will be better.

Diagnosis in the team *is* a continuous process, never complete.

THE TEACHER'S EXPERIENCE

Alone in his classroom, the teacher is already carrying out all the tasks necessary to maintain a learning center. He diagnoses student need, prepares lessons to meet the need, evaluates and records his results. The cycle is repeated many times daily.

But he is not satisfied, nor should he be. No one person can fail to identify more need than he can satisfy. Significant individualization of instruction takes time, energy and expertise beyond the limits of any one of us alone. Unfortunately, asking for and using help are not simple processes at all. Many times they are painful. Matters that were private, subjective, and not always in the individual's own full awareness must now be made public.

In a recent local survey, teachers were asked, "How do you teach? Why do you teach like that? What do you think is the most important in learning?" The fifty teachers answered the first question comfortably but expressed surprise at the "Why?" question and experienced difficulty in explaining why they teach as they do. The value question was avoided by many, and the others were not sure what was most important. Such reaction is fine so long as those who share it do not have to communicate with others. We know that as human beings teachers do have a personal philosophy and a value scale that become involved in every life decision. As teachers they have some sort of behavior model that "explains" why students behave as they do and, therefore, how the teacher needs to behave to modify student behavior. We also know that a perceptive observer can arrive inductively at that teacher's educational objectives simply by watching him at work over a period of time. Therefore, one discovers in every classroom purposeful *teacher behavior* growing out of an unstated value substructure.

Working Together

When the teacher shares responsibility for his students with anyone else, however, these dimensions can no longer remain unstated or ill-defined. Whether the teacher is cooperating with an aide in the classroom, asking certain students to teach each other, sending students to an aide or another teacher in an external learning center, or working cooperatively as a member of a teaching team, all know that:

1. The teacher must put his philosophy into words and must understand the philosophy of his teammates. They must agree upon a general system of priorities to guide their curriculum decisions and must find some means of living comfortably with the inevitable elements of philosophical disagreement.
2. The team must define the objectives toward which they work in sufficient operational detail so that these goals give structure and purpose to the work of everyone on the team.

40

3. The team must develop together a diagnostic-teaching model around which to define their cooperative efforts. The educational objective gives a target for their efforts while the behavior model provides a means for determining relevant and meaningful teaching behavior in terms of the objective. In practice, there is relatively little disagreement on *what* it is we hope to teach a student but frequent disagreement on *how* we get that kid to learn!

4. Given the three elements above, the individual teacher must live with his inadequacy in the more exposed arena. He must experience trust in the team and also must feel trusted by the team in order for this cooperative endeavor to be successful. Such mutual trust develops slowly, . . . often painfully, so the team must accept this part of the process as necessary and inevitable.

5. Given mutual trust, all on the team must rediscover the ultimate wisdom of trusting the child as his own best teacher. Only when the team learns to involve the child in self-diagnosis and decision-making processes concerning his learning will the cooperative effort bear full fruit. Especially in the public schools where large numbers of students are always with us, individualization of instruction is impossible unless the student truly becomes an independent learner, utilizing the resources of the team and the school to further his own self-directed learning.

In a self-contained classroom, the teacher has always had his philosophy, his teaching objectives, his rationale of behavior; sharing these with others and learning to work with others, therefore, should not be difficult. But it is. Expect this process to be difficult and to take time. Plan for it. Pay due attention to the primary teaching task, but don't begrudge the time invested in "group maintenance": the diagnosis of the team's communications processes, the foundations mentioned above on which effective teams are built. As in other

areas of diagnosis, team diagnosis must be continuous and modification of the team operation in response to the diagnosis must be continuous. It all takes time.

Diagnosis and Evaluation in the Learning Center

Although diagnosis does take time, it need not be any more formal or tedious than you as teacher demand, either of yourself or of the situation. You need basically three kinds of feedback: something on the child as a learner, something on yourself, and something on the system.

How to Gather Information on Yourself. You as teacher are probably the biggest learner in any teaching-learning situation. You have the responsibility for guiding children's growth, helping the team effort grow in effectiveness, and perfecting your own skills as a teacher. As learner you need information on yourself to function more efficiently. Where can you gather information on yourself as learner within this learning center framework? From at least three sources: yourself, the children, and other staff members.

From yourself you might find out, through introspective processes, the answers to some of these questions. You may wish to record the answers on tape or to jot them down on paper several different times during the year:

a. What did I most enjoy teaching recently?

b. Where did I feel most comfortable in my teaching lately?

c. When did I close up and become less than I can be in my teaching lately?

d. When did I feel most hostile in my work recently? When did I feel most giving?

e. Am I following any consistent patterns in my teaching? Am I content to follow these patterns or do I want to change?

f. What do I stay away from in my teaching? Any content areas, processes, procedures, media, children, etc.? Should I modify my behavior to include a wider variety of styles in my work?

g. Where do I need more help to improve myself or my work and where can I get this help? Do I want to get it?

h. What is most important to me in my work? Academic areas? Certain skills? Certain behavior? Where am I putting most of my energy these days? Do I want to continue this output of energy or do I wish to go another direction for a while?

It might be interesting to find out how your children and your colleagues would answer the same questions about you. We can see part of our own behavior no one else can see, but, just as certainly, we may hide part of our behavior from ourselves. Others may be able to provide clues about behaviors you have overlooked. Then, of course, there are things about yourself that no one sees clearly yet. This certainly ensures room for learning more about yourself and continuing to grow . . . if you want to grow and learn!

Information about yourself can be found using a variety of techniques and processes. Whatever you are ready for emotionally will determine the process you will want to use. Some of the processes given below may require more emotional guts for you at certain times. You may wish to vary the informational gathering systems to suit you on any particular day. Maybe you want to grow like Jack's beanstalk one day and be reassured completely another. You know that children's growth isn't straight line or continuously all out. Why should yours be?

a. *Tape or video-tape recorders.* One way to get information about your behavior as teacher, as team member, or in your work with parents is to tape record or video-tape record a segment of your actions. This taping may consist of nothing more elaborate than setting up the cameras and just letting them run or turning the camera on the class and recording children's behavior while you work. You may wish to play back these sessions by yourself, with a friend or teammate, or with the children. You can compare your reactions with those of other adults and with those of the children involved in the session. How do they see what you have done? How did they feel?

b. *Analogies.* Sometimes children may not wish to give you direct feedback about how they are viewing you as a teacher. They may feel more free to answer some of the following questions about you in analogous fashion:
    1. What animal do I remind you of today?
    2. If I were a color, what color would I be today?
    3. What kind of weather would I be?
    4. What bird, water, kind of sea, landscape, etc., would I be?
    5. If I went to a costume party, how would I dress?
    6. What story character do I remind you of?

c. *Time chart.* Keeping track of the time you allot to certain activities and the sequence in which you teach may help you to see patterns in your behaviors and what you may be leaving out of your teaching.

d. *Feedback from children.* Feedback from children may be as simple as having them write, draw or tell the answer or answers to questions you may have about your teaching. You may ask them what they think you are teaching well, or not so well, what changes they see in you, what particularly they have responded to favorably or unfavorably in the way you are working lately, or the answer to any other question you want to know about yourself and your teaching.

e. *Team questionnaires.* Adults with whom you work may provide answers to some of these same questions. Once a team develops trust, exchanges of this sort are very useful.

How to Gather Information About Children. Information gathered about children may be for your use, for the use of other learning team members, for that of a group of children, or for individual children. Some of the same processes you used to gather information on yourself could be used for gathering information on youngsters. Other helpful processes may be found in questioning:

a. *What happens when children are grouped in certain ways?* As part of the learning center process, children will be grouped or will group themselves in a variety of ways. What happens to learning and to interpersonal processes for children who are grouped (or group themselves):

  1. By interest or choice patterns, including interest centers, ways of responding (painting, inquiry, writing, etc.)?
  2. By academic ability levels?
  3. By choosing to work with certain children?
  4. By sociometric measures?
  5. By their choice of whom they wish to teach them for the day or the period?

6. By teacher choice of students the teacher wishes to work with?

7. By learning styles, including different sensory patterns (visual, auditory, etc.), problem-solving styles (straight-line thinking styles, multilevel or multidimensional thinking styles), wish for longer or shorter work times, desire to work alone or in groups, and so forth?

8. By allowing children who wish to teach to choose their group?

b. *How may information about children be recorded?* In addition to the traditional recording of information on cumulative records, in grade books, and on report cards, information about children may be recorded in a variety of other ways:

1. Tape or video-tape recording for playing back to children, to parents, or to other team members for a variety of reasons. These recordings could help children define a more accurate (and usually more positive) concept of themselves as learner, as a group member, as a physical person, and as a being operating in particular patterns within a certain learning framework.

2. Teacher recording of impressions of children's academic or interpersonal learnings. These records may be for a single individual (What did Johnny do well during physical education time?) or for a group (How many children are having trouble with *ch* words today?); they may be useful only for a day or two or may be worth including in some more permanent file.

3. Child recording of information about himself for his uses or for teacher's use. Children may wish to record this information in a variety of ways; they may wish to draw, write, record, act out, or record in cartoon fashion answers to such questions as:

What was the most fun for you today?

Where did you have trouble in spelling, reading, etc., today?

With whom did you most enjoy working today?

What questions would you like to ask Mr. Brown today?

How many times did you feel happy today?

What would you like to say to Mrs. Lane today?

4. Other teachers or children record the way they view the learning processes of different children or groups within the learning sequence. This is especially helpful when one teacher wants to concentrate on the teaching process and another can record his impressions of what is happening to children (and to the other teacher).

How to Gather Information on the System. A learning team approach needs feedback at several stages to keep the system functioning efficiently. Recording of this information should take as little effort as possible to facilitate viewing the process over a period of time. If this record keeping becomes an elaborate time-motion study on each child similar to some huge, three-dimensional Monopoly game, then the team may spend so much time planning, charting, recording, stranding, and slow-charting that it may experience total frustration. Could the child chart his own schedule each day? Could he help plan the sequence he will follow and the activities he wants? Maybe you don't even need a chart at all. If your schedules make an airline flight plan look simple, team members, it is possible you are overdoing the recording bit.

Some of the information you may want to get can be obtained from process sessions among team members and with children. There is some research evidence to suggest that children's morale may not be as high as teacher morale in learning centers unless they are actively involved in the planning and evaluating . . . unless, in effect, children are team members, too. Otherwise, they may feel left out or like some type of experimental pawn. Teachers may not realize this because an elaborate learning center design may promote in them feelings of belonging and feelings of worth. When this happens, many of the teacher's needs for appreciation and acceptance, but few of the children's, may be met. These process sessions might include items like the following:

What is important to me now?

How am I feeling about my part in this process?

How am I responding to other team members?

What suggestions do I have to increase learning effectiveness?

Suppose You Are a Learning Team of One. It may be that, much as you would like to be a part of one of these extensive and glorious learning teams, you find yourself a member of a team of one. Is it possible for you to use a learning center concept? To this end you might:

1. "Diagnose" the "learning team" available to you. Might you use the counselor in other ways than grading tests? Do you have a principal who would enjoy teaming once in awhile? Can you get away with "team teaching" some area with the teacher across the hall (regardless of his grade level)? Are there children in your class or other grade levels who can act as teachers or diagnosticians? Can you work with other grade level members or learning projects? Can parents help? Can you team with yourself by using a listening post or pre-recorded video-tape? Are there high school or college volunteers available? What about the custodian and the nurse; do they have skills that would help children to learn? There may be more learning specialists around than you are using. Librarians, speech therapists, district office personnel are really specialist teachers.

2. "Diagnose" the "learning center" space available to you in your classroom. Are you making the most of the space available to you in your classroom? How many other ways can you use space to increase learning efficiency? Can you arrange:

    a. Places for a child to be alone to work?

    b. Areas for groups to work and to be separate from the rest of the class?

    c. Seating arrangements other than chairs, perhaps floors, cushions, mats, benches?

    d. Study carrels, if only three-sided cardboard panels to put in front of any child who wants one?

    e. Spaces where children can work away from your eagle eye?

    f. Equipment set up for work . . . record players with earphones, listening posts, video-tape reruns, slide projectors, cassettes, language masters, tone bells, science equipment?

    g. Areas for children to go to when they want to work on self projects or just think?

3. "Diagnose" the "learning center" space available to you in the rest of the school and in the neighborhood. Are you restricting yourself unnecessarily to the space within your classroom walls? Can you find individual and group working space outside, in the halls, in the multi-purpose room, in the neighborhood? Do the lunch benches have to be used only for eating? How else might they be used?

4. "Diagnose" the effective use of you as a "learning team." Are you doing too much grading of papers that would better be done as a class or by a small group or individual? Are you letting your children help you enough with planning, evaluating, diagnosing, and following through on learning tasks? Are you so in earnest about the diagnose—teach—evaluate process that you forget to relax and enjoy the process and yourself and the children? Do you feel burdened down by the entire responsibility of providing the push for learning in your classroom? You might just be missing the whole point of the entire learning center process.

Discover. All over the United States, your district and your neighborhood are experimenting with learning center designs and concepts. Go visiting. Discover variety.

At Parkview Elementary School in Simi, California, the Learning Center team is made up of a coordinating teacher, two reading specialists, one full-time paid aide and nine primary classroom teachers.

In Goleta, California, a Child Study Team exists in each school to assist the teacher or teaching team in diagnosis and planning. This team includes the school psychologist, nurse, speech therapist and reading specialist with teacher and parent participating when appropriate. The school principal is responsible administratively for the team operation.

In Fountain Valley, California, the school district has built the learning center into the initial building design.

Summary

Whatever the level of complexity of design or staffing, learning centers are attempts to individualize instruction for more effective education for children. They deserve to exist only if evaluation shows that more effective education does result. Individualization requires continuous diagnosis, continuous modification of program to meet diagnosed need, and evaluation of effect (more diagnosis) to start the cycle again. Diagnosis in this context broadens to include assessment of teacher needs and strengths and diagnosis of the system itself as well as the child. Because these are cooperative efforts, more formal definition must be given the philosophy and purpose we once took for granted. In this process, we should note that decision-making is shared in many ways and has been pushed lower in the school hierarchy. As students assume more responsibility for their own learning processes, they will need to reassure the teacher that all is going well; teachers must in turn reassure the principal, who cannot possibly keep track of all that is going on in his school. The principal in turn. . . . But that's all right. Responsibility *must* be reversed if the learning center activities are to be the healthy "people processes" that deserve a place in your school.

Children on their own— centers and stations for learning

Margaret Fennel, Principal
Elizabeth Kelly, Supervisor
Robert Frost Elementary School
New Carrollton, Maryland

Some major goals of today's elementary schools are greater self-motivation, self-direction and the personalization of instruction. The Learning Station and Learning Center concept appears to be one way to achieve these goals.

Individualizing learning and teaching with stations is an alternative to the traditional concept of seatwork, in which children stay at their desks all or most of the time using ditto sheets or working from the chalkboard. This approach gives some choice of activities each day. Children assume more responsibility for self-direction which includes recording and evaluating their own progress once the activities are completed. In this flexible environment, children's enthusiasm is reflected in their attitudes and in their work.

LR means "Language Related"—a chance to choose. Involvement with a purpose enhances self-motivation and self-direction.

A well-organized center: carefully planned and executed— clear, legible directions. Materials ready; pockets hold keys for self-correcting.

Children move with a purpose to the next assignment. They're *not* too young to be responsible.

"Where do I go next?" Problem solving involves children. Directions are important. Listen!

Interesting content (in this instance, Science) provides motivation for self-direction.

The center is about "Syllables." There's space to work, place for materials, a comfortable atmosphere. The result: productivity.

A corridor wall serves as the location for a station that requires putting together a puzzle map of the United States. Stations need not demand written answers.

Real-life materials make the application of skills a lot more fun.

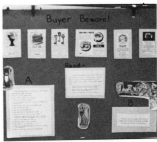

Another center—this time it's about paragraphs.

Space to work, variety in choice, and help near by are a requisite for learning.

An ordinary cardboard box covered with Contact paper becomes the location for four stations or a total learning center.

A colorful but simple station reinforces this youngster's knowledge of beginning consonants—much more interesting than a ditto sheet. In the background is a chart that assigns Math stations.

If reading and listening are difficult, perhaps visualization will give the message.

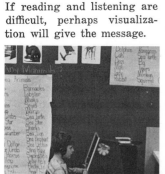

Materials are close at hand and easy to obtain.

In the corridor again—with an aide this time—working at a center on comprehension that includes several stations of increasing difficulty.

A change of scenery helps; besides, there's no other place or posture that serves to complete the job.

Helpful hardware

Arthur M. Enzmann, Director
Department of Early Childhood Education
Detroit Public Schools

5

Historically, teachers have not reacted favorably toward urgings to use the fruits of technology in their teaching procedures. Those who think nothing about stepping into a high-powered multigadgeted automobile and zooming out into overloaded expressways rear back in terror at the thought of having to manipulate a mechanical contrivance in the classroom. Today this attitude is constantly challenged. The advent of the increased availability of supplemental federal funding for the purchase of educational equipment has meant the focusing of attention of an increasing number of industrial concerns upon this potentially lucrative field.

EFFECTIVE UTILIZATION

In those instances in the past when teachers have sought to use such rather simple devices as the motion picture projector and the filmstrip projector, their methods were generally unsound. For reasons known best by the individual

teacher, it was often assumed that when she went to the bother of setting up the motion picture projector and screen and obtaining the films, as many children as possible should watch the film at the same time. It was quite generally assumed, also, that learning resulted from watching the films, and that information presented in this manner was automatically integrated into the learner's experiential background. Remember the many justifications made for the continuance of "movie day" in the school program? This was the day when all the children trooped to a centrally located darkened room to watch a series of films, many of which had no relationship to the materials being studied at the time or any relationship to each other. How secure we were in our belief that we were employing modern educational techniques! That it was convenient for one teacher to monitor a very large group of children, thus allowing some of the teachers who had brought their classes to the movie room to slip away and return to their rooms to correct papers and pin up bulletin boards, may have had some import also. This procedure may have had some value when children did not have home television and equated the motion picture with cowboys and Indians and Saturday matinee series, and it appeared appropriate to convert this medium to an instructional tool. Unfortunately, even though the times have changed, our use of this type of audiovisual material frequently retains its horse-and-buggy approach.

Modern educational theories place a heavy emphasis upon breaking down the lock-step rigidity of our instructional program. Emphasis upon individualization of instruction has resulted in teachers giving thought to the fact that all children do not need the same experiences at the same time and that the varied learning styles of children indicate the need for a concomitant variety in instructional styles. The proper planned use of instructional technology offers the teacher considerable assistance in meeting this need.

Experience has shown that elementary school students, even those in the lower grades, are less terrorized by technology than their teachers. Having grown up in an age in which the fantastic marvels of technocracy are accepted as routine and quite predictable, they accept the use of the products of this technocracy in a routine and non-threatened way. Teachers should take advantage of this degree of sophistication on the part of the students to involve them in the personal direction of their learning program. This can be done by setting aside a portion of the room for individual and small-group use of audiovisual materials. Students can be taught to operate the equipment in a relatively short period of time, and if care is taken to do this adequately, the equipment will not suffer any wear beyond that to be expected by normal teacher use. Having children operate the equipment properly is only an intermediary objective, however; the ultimate objective is to have the child use the equipment as a means of expanding his education.

INSTRUCTIONAL UNITS

Many if not most teachers are convinced that children learn best when they become involved in large units of instruction rather than in discrete, isolated instructional lessons. Integration and internalization of learning on the part of the student are more easily accomplished when the student is able to see how daily and weekly activities fit into a larger pattern of learning. There is no single avenue to knowledge and wisdom; the more ways a child learns to approach a problem the higher the success potential of that child. The unit approach seeks to attain this broad objective and thus naturally draws upon as many different resources as possible to spur learning, e.g., basic texts, supplementary texts, pictures, resource persons, group discussions and the kinds of audiovisual materials that require the use of "helpful hardware."

Let us picture for a moment what a contemporary elementary classroom might look like during part of the day. Presuming that the class has become involved in a unit of study centering on some social studies or science concept, we could see the following types of activities taking place. Several children might be engaged in research on the topic using the basic texts plus materials gathered from libraries and additional sources. Several children might be preparing art work to illustrate certain aspects of the concept under study. Another small group may be viewing a filmstrip which they located from a catalogue of available audiovisual materials. A fourth group might be preparing a taped report accompanied by a series of transparencies which they will later share with the rest of the class.

An obvious implication of this scene is that the teacher recognizes the importance of multisensory learning and has structured her classroom in such a way that children may use many different learning modalities. Making use of "helpful hardware" and its well-designed software has in this instance multiplied the effectiveness of the instructional program by its additional dimensions.

A common problem faced by most teachers who group children for instruction is how to deal with two or more groups at the same time in an instructionally sound manner. This is especially difficult with young children because their independent reading ability seldom measures up to their ability to work independently in other ways.

There are many ways in which hardware can help the teacher as she attempts to resolve this dilemma. Let us examine some of the alternatives available to her as she plans

independent activities for one group while she offers direct reading instruction to another. These activities during the reading period should support and reinforce the reading program in a constructive and worthwhile manner. The least desirable alternative is to provide reams of paperwork that have little variety, little interest, and in truth provide little learning. We all are familiar with the different ways in which children handle assignments of this nature. Some find the work difficult, and when the teacher is not available for questioning the child sits and ponders, or just plain sits, following an unsuccessful effort to complete the task. On the other end, the quick responder is barely back to his seat with the hectographed material when he is finished—the lines are drawn, the blanks filled in, the sentences copied. He has learned little that was new and is now ready for more. What he frequently gets is more of the same, an additional sheet or two to complete. Of course, we carefully label the added work as enrichment or broadening, but is it?

An alternative procedure is to study the total language arts curriculum and by following this study determine what aspects could be handled by the children on an independent basis. Suppose the teacher realizes on the basis of her curriculum review that the vital study of literature is being short-changed because of a heavy emphasis upon reading skill development. It would appear that this lack of balance in language arts instruction could be rectified in a way that would solve the teacher's dilemma as to what group two will do when she is working with group one, plus providing the advantage of a sound use of pupil time in a way that will effectively support the teacher's activities.

HARDWARE ACTIVITIES

Let us suppose that the teacher is developing a lesson dealing with a basic reading skill with one group of children. The other children could be working in another part of the room on any of the following activities: (1) listening to a story record while seated at a listening station. Many types of listening stations with multiple earphones are now available at moderate prices. If the earphones are not available, the children can listen directly to a softly playing phonograph or tape recorder. Research has shown that exposure to the oral presentation of good literature is a strong component of a good language program. A regular exposure to good literature contributes directly to growth in many skills, habits, and attitudes. Thus, this group, although not under the direct supervision of the teacher, is involved in a long range meaningful activity.

An additional small group activity which contributes to literature exposure is (2) the viewing of a literature filmstrip. A large variety of good filmstrips are now on the market for purchase or loan. The filmstrip projector is simple to operate and the picture may be projected in a lighted room. Because only a small group of children will be watching it at one time it is not necessary to get a very large picture. In fact, keeping the picture small, using a two-foot piece of white paper taped to the side of a file cabinet, contributes to the feeling of intimacy of the group with a resultant increase in cooperative spirit.

Another piece of hardware available in many classrooms for use by the second group is (3) the television set. Unfortunately the use of television as an instructional tool has been sidetracked by secondary issues and arguments. Not the least of these is the very threatening assertion by its more enthusiastic proponents that TV has the capability of teaching some materials better and more cheaply, and thus may be the potential replacement of the trained teacher. Early emphases appeared to be almost entirely on large group instruction with the number of students sometimes going up into the hundreds in one sitting. When many of the original claims could not be substantiated, the whole idea of televised instruction received a setback from which it has never really recovered.

Teachers on the whole still apply the same concept to TV that they applied to the early use of the motion picture: if it was good for one child to see it, why not show it to all at the same time? May I suggest an alternative approach? Let's use the TV as another kind of small group activity. There are more problems to be faced when TV is used as a supplementary teaching tool for independent student groups. The major one revolves about the coordination of room instructional plans and the scheduling of programs to be broadcast. Normally, however, the same type of program, e.g., storyland, etc., has a regular time slot each week. Frequently certain programs will have regular repeat broadcasts during a single week thus increasing the flexibility of program usage. The shared intimacy of the small viewing group greatly enhances the learning to be derived over that which goes on when a whole roomful of children are seated at their desks watching a particular program.

THE LEARNING LABORATORY

During the spring of 1969, I visited a sixth-grade classroom to discuss curriculum with a young man teacher. This was a follow-up of a visit which had taken place about three years previously. At that time he had been experiencing considerable difficulty in developing a learning environment in his classroom. The children were frequently apathetic, often hostile, and usually uninterested in forwarding their education. The young teacher truly desired to do a good job and was frustrated when his efforts brought forth so little response from the students. With the encouragement and support of his administration, he decided that he was going to interest his students in learning or exhaust himself in the attempt.

The first premise he adopted was that the traditional textbook, basal-reader approach did not offer sufficient inspiration to his students to bring about their personal involvement in their learning program.

A second premise was that no single package of materials or equipment, no matter how brilliantly advertised, would solve the wide variety of learning problems he encountered in his room. It was going to be necessary for him to review

many materials, dig into available research, and finally develop and construct as many of the items that he wanted and needed as possible. Working with the students in his class, he constructed several sets of plyboard study carrels. They bought some inexpensive electronic tape recorder components and several headsets. They held a bake sale and other fund-raising drives to buy materials and equipment they could not construct. As this was going on, class attitudes began to change, students began to feel that they were constructing and working in a learning laboratory. They soon began to visualize a broader variety of equipment. The school parent-teacher association recognized the interest and enthusiasm of the students and voted to support the project with sufficient money to allow purchase of several additional pieces of equipment, a cassette tape recorder, a Craig Reader, and a filmstrip projector. The school system provided a television and a phonograph.

The students working with the teacher decided on what materials they needed to obtain in order to meet the curriculum needs of their sixth-grade class. The catalogues of the audiovisual department of the school system and local library were consulted and materials borrowed with regularity.

All of these efforts were not accomplished during the first year. Each succeeding class became part of the project, making its personal contribution to the organization and reorganization of the learning centers in the room. Previous students now in junior high school come back to help after school and, through the indication of their interest, build the interest and cooperative spirit of the new sixth-grade students.

What a change has occurred! Formerly disinterested students now help design a learning program that they need. They approach problems from a variety of ways and realize that self-direction along with self-control has been given to them. The teacher finds his energy being used in helping students program their learning instead of, as previously, in a futile attempt to maintain order and "cover the material."

The hardware alone is, of course, not the answer. But it does provide the avenue for change in teaching strategy. It can affect the educational climate of the classroom in a very positive manner. As in the case described above, it may make the difference between a sterile, increasingly remote learning environment and a viable, dynamic one.

COMPUTER ASSISTED INSTRUCTION

We have discussed briefly a way of making technology contribute to the instructional program by the programming of several relatively unsophisticated pieces of equipment into the activities of a classroom. Looming on the horizon and already in use in a few school districts are pieces of equipment so sophisticated that they outstrip our current ability to successfully cope with them. Leading the way in this area are the several basic systems of computer assisted instruction (CAI).

Although the mechanical approaches to the various CAI systems may vary, all are based upon an attempt to increase the individualization of instruction for students at all grade and ability levels. The systems operating today generally suffer from the fact that the hardware has outpaced our ability to create the software or curriculum material which will adequately meet our needs. The computer can easily store the curriculum data fed into it and upon demand can bring the data to the student in a sure, almost instantaneous manner. The problem is, however, do we know what data we want to bring swiftly to the student? Many programs operating today are simply an updating of materials developed during the honeymoon period of the teaching machine fad of the early 1960's. These materials were based upon a somewhat naive assumption that conceptual learning is analogous to walking to the store, that all you had to do was to point the learner in the right direction and have him take steps toward it. The steps might be large or small, depending upon the capabilities of the student, but the destination remained the same and usually the route used was the same for all. Some of our very sophisticated CAI equipment today is still programmed to use this linear approach. In these cases all we have is a very expensive education toy. Other school systems are attempting to refine this approach to accommodate a variety of branching techniques that will offer instructional alternatives to students as they proceed through the programs.

Let no educator underestimate the problems involved in the task of foreseeing and accounting for the many variables in individual learning styles. The glamorous computer is completely dependent upon the less glamorous, and indeed often prosaic programmer, and therein lies the problem. As the programmers themselves characterize the problem, "garbage in—garbage out."

Much research needs to be done in this field and a large proportion of this research must be longitudinal in nature. Short-term research has repeatedly demonstrated that significant short-term gains can be achieved by almost any new technique. Whether these short-term gains can be maintained over the long haul remains to be seen. For example, many educators question the long-range effectiveness of the reinforcing devices used in computer assisted instruction. How long will the student respond favorably to the figurative pat on the back that the computer gives him when he achieves a correct answer? How many variations on a theme can the computer produce to keep reinforcement novel to the student? These are only minor issues compared to those of determining the content of the computer curriculum and the best way of tapping the computer's data bank.

Examined positively, CAI does offer the student another way of learning and can strongly support the school's instructional program by offering sources of information not readily available in the school setting. It can be used to stimulate students to set their own paces for learning and to allow those who are inspired to do so an opportunity to research areas only skimmed in the average classroom setting.

Hardware offers teachers the opportunity to increase student involvement in learning by adding to the variety of experiences available, thus contributing toward the improvement of cooperative student interaction in a way that may spice the often bland fare we present to our classes.

Those wide open spaces

Gudrun Dewar, Coordinator
Intermediate Grades
Vancouver, British Columbia, Canada

Of all the innovations since Sputnik gathered educators into orbit, none has caused more excitement, more interest, or more questioning than the open area teaching concept. Learning theories dating from the time when messages were inscribed on the walls of caves to our own era of multimedia technology can all be tried in the unique setting of the open type school.

How is this possible? How does it evolve in practice?

SPACE AND ACOUSTICS

Based on the principle of flexibility in instructional procedures, the structural plans of open area school buildings provide for the accommodation of large numbers of children

in large work spaces allowing for various groupings and re-groupings of pupils under the direction of teacher teams. The work areas differ in sizes according to need, some being equal to a double classroom whereas others are comparable to ten classrooms. The fascinating variations in shape are both functional and pleasing to the eye: triangular, circular, octagonal, L-shaped, or rectangular, according to the design of the building. Spaces are linked by corridors or short stairways and are referred to as pods, decks, or areas rather than rooms, divisions, or classes.

Some building designers have provided moveable interior walls that may partly or entirely screen off sections of the large open space. Others have made provision for such walls to be installed when and if they should become necessary. Some traditional school buildings, when faced with the need for expansion, are given an addition that is open area in design. The open area in such schools sometimes houses the primary children, while in other instances the intermediate pupils are in the new quarters.

Acoustics play a highly significant role in the success of open area teaching. Not all but most open areas are carpeted with acoustical floor coverings of synthetic and sturdy material in a wide variety of colorings. Soft greens, strong blues, warm golds and vivid rusts make for an attractive and inviting setting for learning. Color is not the only factor in the use of carpeting. Children sit or lie full length on the rug surface at times when the grouping is small. The cold hard surfaces of traditional classrooms do not lend themselves to this easy and natural informality. Color and cushioned floor surfaces take second place, however, to the effectiveness of space itself, one of the chief advantages in the physical arrangements of the open learning center.

Acoustical treatment of floors relieves the clatter of scraping chairs, dropped books and pencils, plus the tread of many feet. When treatment is applied also to ceilings, the amount, educators and architects have discovered, has to be carefully gaged. Only in this way can extremes of atmosphere be avoided.

FURNISHINGS FOR ACTIVITIES

The main furnishings in open area schools consist of small tables with a shelf for the all-important tote tray—sturdy, lightweight, and colorful—that each pupil uses for transporting his instructional materials. Trapezoidal tables prove useful in making possible many arrangements for group work.

Art and science activities are sometimes carried on in a "wet" space—uncarpeted and adjacent to or part of the main area. The resource center or library is located in some schools in the center of the open area, in others in a nearby wing. Individual study carrels are proving their worth as pupils make use of them for independent work and special assignments; their side partitions provide a measure of privacy in contrast to the roundtable sessions where interaction is used in the learning process.

Landscaped courtyards with simple platforms for dramatic presentations are frequently incorporated into open area school designs. Music centers, not usually part of the main area, are self-contained rooms often of an unusual shape and with carpeted tiers providing seating accommodation.

Audio-visual aids are much in evidence in open type schools, particularly the tape recorder, the overhead projector, and the listening post. Storage facilities are being constantly assessed and improved upon; accessibility without sacrificing the gains made by the effectiveness of space is the aim. Chalkboard space is generally limited, and displays have to be arranged with discretion to avoid a cluttered effect. A present desirable trend is for architects and educators to sit together on new building committees in an effort to incorporate the best ideas for teaching convenience, structural soundness, and artistic appearance.

GROUPING FOR LEARNING

Assuming that acoustics and physical arrangements of the area are satisfactory, what can be expected from teachers and pupils functioning there? What improvements in the general learning pattern may be found?

Perhaps the greatest single benefit that the open area plan confers is the facility for regrouping. Large group to small group, small group to subgroup, dismissals and assemblies can all be managed in a minimum of time. Social behavior under these conditions can be readily observed and by more than one person. The growth in mature bearing is noted as freedom of movement, combined with responsibility, is put into practice. In some instances where this growth is not immediately apparent, and a child seems ill-suited to the open area way of school life, a request for a transfer to a more formal learning center is granted. In such cases, a request to return to the open area often appears a short time later. The visitor feels much less of an intruder in the spacious learning center and can circulate with ease giving help to an individual child or joining a group activity. Again maturity is evident among the pupils as visiting adults are treated as naturally as their peers.

69

Another major advantage is the opportunity for teachers to work as a team to improve instruction. It is possible to share not only the space but the pupils, the activities, and the resources. Together they can organize their program, select materials, prepare teaching aids, and evaluate the pupils' progress and their own efforts.

Experienced team members in open area schools offer these viewpoints about this way of teaching:

They can get all the children involved in a learning situation.

They have opportunity to do more in an area of competence while being released from an area in which they feel less competent.

They enjoy the opportunity to talk over and share problems.

They see a startling improvement in attitude and progress when pupils are working in small groups.

They see noticeable gains among all pupils in their ability to work independently.

They say they find themselves changing, in outlook and in personality as they interact with other members of their team.

Most teams function best with a team leader. Status is not a requisite in many cases where a sharing of this role on a rotation basis is preferred.

What types of teachers find success and satisfaction in a setting where group-oriented guidance for children is the pattern of instruction? Those with a pioneering spirit, perhaps, who like new ventures. Age and experience seem relatively unimportant considerations when weighed against compatibility. Open area teachers recognize this as the most essential team member trait. Where teams exist, team planning must exist also. Ingenuity must be used to find time for the interchange of ideas, for arranging the schedule, for deciding who is to introduce a topic, who is to help and in what manner with follow-up activities. Is the subject matter load to be shared or are the children to be shared? When and how become vital questions in every aspect of team planning. Teachers confess they find themselves changing long established viewpoints as the team power becomes a favorable force. Finding the necessary moments for team planning and evaluating progress presents one of the greatest challenges in open area teaching. Most planning is done after school hours, but short, extra team meetings are often possible. Some well established open area learning centers have reached the stage where pupils are able to carry on independently for the first half hour of the school day, while team members brief each other on their specific responsibilities for the remainder of the day.

MEETING DISTRACTIONS

In initial stages of open area development, teachers advocate short term objectives, with flexible scheduling and easily changed arrangements. Despite acoustical treatment of floors and ceilings, there can be considerable sound distraction of children's and teachers' voices. How much noise can pupils tolerate around them as they work? Marguerite Henry, able author and delightful speaker, shed some light on this concern in her remarks at the 1969 ACEI Study Conference. She said that as a child when concentrating on her first story efforts seated at the old farmhouse kitchen table, she could work comfortably only when accompanied by the voices of her mother and the hired girl working around her.

Open area teachers who are sensitive to noise distraction occasionally flash the ceiling lights on and off as a signal to all to moderate their voices. Other teachers prefer to forestall noise volume that exceeds tolerance levels by arranging for quiet activities with some pupils while the others are engaged in lively learning situations. Pupils who are easily distracted by sound have opportunity to use the study carrels or the small conference rooms.

A child in difficulty can be more readily helped over a learning hurdle in the open area than in the enclosed classroom. He need not be made conspicuous before his peers. Similarly the show-off does not easily find an audience for his antics. The climate for learning is a more natural and a more comfortable one for every child.

How are pupils evaluated in open area schools? A card system is common, with a card for each pupil containing brief comments plus a memorandum of specific troubles he is encountering. Books and materials used are listed as well as results of quizzes and check-up tests. Often pupils are trained to keep a plan book of their own, writing down their assignments under the appropriate date. With the interchange of groupings throughout the day, such information is helpful to both pupil and teacher.

In all types of learning centers there is an increasing tendency to utilize paraprofessional help to free the teacher from routine tasks. Open area settings, because of the ease of movement, are particularly suited to the employment of teacher aides. Open area teachers are very grateful for this type of assistance. It not only helps to gain added team planning time, but enables them to give undivided attention to small groups and individuals in much more measure than when acting alone.

One interesting but not really surprising result of the open area school experiment has been the attempt on the part of teachers and principals to institute team teaching and flexible groups within the traditional school. Those who

have met with success say, "What is it the open area school can do that cannot be done in our school?" The answer is twofold. In the first place, it is people who create the learning climate regardless of the structural details of the environment. In the second place, the same things *can* be done in the traditional school, but so much more conveniently in the open area.

Is the open area teaching concept likely to take a permanent hold? In decision making it has already been noted that many of the difficulties of operation are those that plague any type of learning center. Such factors as pupil-teacher ratio, availability of teaching materials, and crowded quarters affect all learning situations.

The open area plan is the nearest approach to date in bringing the child's world into the school room. Possibly the most impressive feature to a visitor is the naturalness of the environment.

In one charming episode shown in the film, "And Sow Tomorrow,"[1] prepared by the Toronto Board of Education, the camera focuses on two little six-year-olds seated side by side at a table, obviously involved in a learning assignment. They are using a few of these moments in solemn and careful assessment of recently acquired open spaces in each other's small mouths. The commentator reminds the audience that this, too, is learning.

John Holt, in *How Children Learn*,[2] asks teachers to give children help and guidance, to listen respectfully when they feel like talking. He suggests further that teachers then "get out of the way." Getting out of the way can be done in a figurative sense only, within the tight confines of the small classroom. It can be done both figuratively and literally in the wide open spaces of the multiclass learning center.

---

1. "And Sow Tomorrow," narrated by Lloyd Dennis. Toronto Board of Education Teaching Aids Department, 1969. Color film, 29 minutes.

2. London: Sir Isaac Pitman and Sons Ltd., 1967, p. 189.

Dimensions of freedom

T. Darrell Drummond, Principal
Lake Normandy School
Potomac, Md.

Lake Normandy School, Potomac, Maryland, designed by John Shaver, attempts to provide open spaces. Three classrooms of five-classroom clusters can be seen in this view.

Children have freedom to work and move about anywhere within the building. The staff believes that learning must be internalized and sometimes this must be done alone.

Class spaces are organized around individual centers designed to develop a skill or expand a concept.

For the most part children are freed from the lock-step of "class progress" to range among the centers and to work at their own level and pace.

With or without the teacher a sense of informality and companionship is part of the experience.

As children gain skill and independence in pursuing learning experiences on their own, the teacher gains time to reflect on her own priorities of who needs her most, or what comes next.

Confidence in one's self precedes an understanding of the dimensions of freedom.

The teacher's structure of learning experiences sets the limits. This card index serves as a self check of time and activities engaged in by the child. The child needs this security as he experiences freedom.

The wealth of materials skillfully structured with many learning centers permit great flexibility in accommodating the needs of the individual learner within the broad range of multi-age classes.

Learning out of bounds

Leslie P. Evans, Director
Office of Special Projects, School of Education
Texas Christian University, Fort Worth, Texas

7

Our revered little Red School House has made way for contemporary structures of glass, aluminum and steel, but environmental structure has not been updated to parallel physical structure. Construction still conforms to nature's method of lighting and to the region's pattern of prevailing winds, bypassing seemingly expensive lighting and environmental comfort control. Old educational patterns frequently prevail inside the precast concrete walls, and many of those reading these lines would still feel comfortable in the current first-grade curriculum as well as in the current curriculum of a favorite history class of bygone high school days.

Not only are the plan and program inflexible, the social structure supporting it remains rigid. School is still a compulsory activity. A child must attend or have his parents face the courts. The buildings may be those in which an-

cestors started their educational careers, or newer ones with rectangular crate-type construction divided, like Sing Sing, into cells, each of which is ruled by a teacher who shuts the door on the outside world. The children still line up—boys in one line, girls in another—and march to the lunchroom, march to the drinking fountain, march to the playground.

WHEN SCHOOL WALLS FALL DOWN!

Fortunately, this picture is not of all the schools in the United States. Educational frontiersmen exist; there are creative principals; there are professional teachers who utilize the total community-environment resources to offset a highly regimented social organization. Even with its monolithic ladder offering a single type of education to all the children of all the people, there is hope for the school if the use of community cultural and education resources is extended outside the school walls.

Learning outside the school walls frees the child from architecturally monotonous classrooms where he may be held captive during sterile class exchanges. On the other hand, the opportunities to learn are all around him; the newspaper and the telephone offices, the radio and television stations, the airport, the bakery, the ice plant, the zoo, the botanical garden, the aquarium, the herpetarium, the museum, the city cultural center, the symphony, the orchestra, the repertory theater. All these and more are open and living textbooks waiting to be read with diligence by the pupil if the utilization of the community resources is carefully and profitably planned. In the classroom there are open textbooks, but few living textbooks! Most of those which are available have been selected by adults on the basis of adult interests. The pervading philosophy is to select reading materials that are "good" for the child or that should develop "taste for good literature." Too often the selection and presentation of materials are made before the student has acquired the necessary skills and speed in reading that make reading profitable and exciting. There must be some means of making school life as exciting as the outside world appears to the budding dropout.

Many educators believe that living and learning outside the school walls make it exciting to live in today's world. Never before have so many amazing discoveries occurred in so many fields of endeavor. Most of these discoveries, either directly or indirectly, are contributing to the highest standard of living ever known. Yet in spite of these material gains the aesthetic and cultural needs of the child are not being cared for as they should be. In the past, man has utilized his wealth to meet the aesthetic needs of a small segment of his posterity. Today it would appear that he has reached the point in civilization whereby all youth can have access to the educational and cultural resources of the community. This is a most difficult problem for a society demanding a solution to the challenge of "educating all of the children of all of the people." This is not a new demand; its intensity, however, has been brought into focus by the many social and technological changes that our nation is experiencing. Youthful protest, racial and ethnic clashes, and the drastic increase in the demand for more and better educated people have caused the educational leader to look beyond the limits of the traditional classroom for a source of aid in educating the potential dropout who does not conform to the conventional type of educational program.

COMMUNITY RESPONSIBILITY EXERCISED

It is evident that many school systems have acknowledged the cultural needs of the youth of the community and have launched promising attacks on this pressing educational problem. Such school systems have shouldered the heavy responsibility for finding solutions to these problems and are being helped by their partners in the home, the community and the nation. More and more educational leaders believe that such a combination, in partnership, can overcome some of the social and cultural practices that tend to stunt the growth of the individual, to keep him from finding

78

joy and satisfaction in his schooling and training, and thus to deny him the right to develop to his satisfactory level of achievement.

The increasing concern for the total education of the nation's children and youth has prompted movements such as the Ford Foundation's funding of the Great Cities Projects and the federal funding of the Elementary and Secondary Education Act of 1965 to encourage the development of exemplary school and community projects which are now making important changes in the lives of children. In his study, *Enrichment of the Cultural Life of the Student Beyond the Traditional School Program,* William R. Haney (1) has reported exemplary programs in many areas, and additional research has revealed others.

Philadelphia. The Philadelphia schools concentrate efforts in activities designed to bring children into direct contact with the cultural, civic and social institutions located in the area where they live. The children are able to meet people who have made important contributions to the arts, sciences, and social services. Opportunities are afforded to the children to develop physical strength and skill in athletic activities. Efforts are also made to help children to develop an appreciation for the fine and performing arts.

Perhaps the most important feature of the Philadelphia improvement program is the on school time in-service teacher training program. During the time teachers are receiving this training, their classes participate in a literature program rich in story-telling, literature films, filmstrips, and recordings. Additional library and special enrichment books have been purchased to support the structured literature program.

Where the desired enrichment program cannot be brought to the school, groups of children are taken to the place of performances. Drama and music groups have been brought to students and efforts are being made to increase such performances. Afterschool activities include experiences in physical fitness activities, bus trips, leisure time hobbies, arts and crafts, musical expression, dramatics, exploratory mathematics and science, and creative writing.

Chicago. The Chicago school system concentrates on meeting the needs of the individual, and widening the cultural horizons of culturally deprived children receives a considerable amount of the school board's attention. The services of a cultural coordinator, special programs in schools, music ensembles, free bus trips and free tickets for special events, cultural opportunities and clubs, as well as leadership training opportunities, are characteristic of other services provided. Auxiliary services and cooperating agencies provide assistance in other areas such as health, recreation, tutorial, guidance and counseling. (3)

St. Louis. To combat the effects of cultural deprivation in the Banneker District, St. Louis, Missouri, and to provide children with experiences to build on in successive grades, field trips are planned: a supermarket, Wonder Bakery, Grant's Farm, the art museum, museum of science and natural history, a "dine-out," Easter Farm, St. Louis Zoo, tour of riverfront, museum of transport, survey tour of

St. Louis, the Chevrolet Plant, KSD Television Station and *Post Dispatch*, the Homer Phillips Hospital, and "Operation Cafeteria." (4)

Detroit. A philosophy of the Detroit schools is that one of the most obvious and perhaps the most successful way to enrich and expand the background of a child is to put him on a bus and take him to places he has never seen and perhaps has never heard of. In keeping with this philosophy, one hundred schools made approximately four hundred bus trips to industrial plants, business establishments, and cultural centers in the school year. In addition, there are walking trips to the fire department, the service station, the supermarket, and trips by private car for smaller groups. Camp experiences are enjoyed by sixth- and seventh-graders. To encourage these trips, busses and bus drivers are maintained for the sole purpose of providing transportation for field trip experiences for the school year.

An interesting feature of the Detroit program is the purchase of paperback books for resale at cost to school children and their parents. The books cover classics in literature, fairy tales, nursery stories, and adventure stories. This practice provides encouragement to the establishment of the habit of reading. Further, teachers are encouraged to search out and recommend newer, more effective instructional materials and methods. Through greater involvement of public and private agencies, a heavy concentration of their resources and personnel has assisted the Detroit schools to successfully attack the problems of the cultural enrichment. (5)

San Diego. One of the most fascinating programs that enables the child to "Learn Out of Bounds" is the San Diego, California, program. The Education Section of the San Diego Zoo encompasses studies for preschool through college level students, both academic and non-academic. In the Children's Zoo, a full-time teacher conducts guided tours for kindergarten, first-grade, and handicapped children. Bus tours are provided for all second-grade students in the county of San Diego, and live animal presentations are seen and heard by all fourth- fifth- and sixth-grade students in the city and by many such grades in the county. A Saturday program in animal study is conducted for secondary students. Courses on a college level, and accredited through a local college, are also taught on the zoo grounds.

Animal sketching, special study series, and the development of film strips and study prints with commentary are non-academic activities. Other regular school year activities include answering many letters of inquiry, conferring with teachers and students, talking to various parents, schools, and service club groups. (6)

Fort Worth. Educators, civic leaders, and cultural organizations in Fort Worth and surrounding areas have combined efforts with Project Change, an ESEA Title III funded project, in developing programs designed to enhance education and the arts. (7)

The Amon Carter Museum of Western Art and the Kimbell Art Foundation have joined together in conducting one full semester of college-level training for persons who will serve as tour guides to direct school children and the public through those facilities.

A similar volunteer guide study program has been initiated at the Fort Worth Zoo. Because of the zoo's tremendous potential for learning and extending school curricular programs, more sophisticated plans for use of the facility are being made. The Project is also working with the director to increase membership in the zoological society.

A one-semester Teacher Training Series was established, in which each of twenty-two community resources provided information and instruction concerning the purposes and uses of its facilities. This series was a major step forward, growing out of the first meeting of administrative heads of the city's cultural organizations for any purpose other than funding or audience building. Response from the teachers and the organizational leaders has been overwhelmingly enthusiastic, with both groups calling for repetition and in-depth continuation.

An annual resource handbook is being compiled, with each of the twenty-two organizations contributing information relating its programs to the school curriculum. The handbook will be distributed to teachers and administrators in the region's school districts, the first material concerning local community and cultural resources to be compiled for the classroom teacher.

A survey of community relations to the arts was conducted by the Project, relating especially to the theater in a ten-county region. Resulting recommendations have led to plans by which a professional Fort Worth-based drama group will tour the region to give school performances. A major project has been the coordination of special student performances of productions by the Fort Worth Opera Association. Capacity audiences in a 3066-seat house heard "La Traviata" and "Don Pasquale." Both events were heavily attended by groups of school children from throughout the region.

The production of "La Traviata" was underwritten by a private donor, so that tickets could be offered at one dollar each. The Opera Guild voted to underwrite the special performance of "Don Pasquale" as a special project, and the Association's Board of Directors voted to include the special children's performances in their budget for the forthcoming year. The Guild will assume the responsibility of sponsoring the activity.

The children were quite an exciting audience for the performers. They followed the action well and were most demonstrative in their reactions. Not understanding a word sung in "La Traviata," the children nevertheless viewed the stage action as a sort of Gene Autry special without horses. When Violetta is dying of consumption, Alfredo rushes onstage to her side. It is a poignant scene. The children cheered Alfredo's arrival as if it were the coming of the U.S. Cavalry. There was a fight sequence between Alfredo and the Baron, a rival for Violetta's heart, and a scene involving a band of gypsies. Both pleased the audience so much that one small boy wrote, "The best part is when the Baron and Alfredo had a fight and the Gyps come in." "The part at the end was the part I liked best. Where that lady died," penned another youthful hand.

For the 1969 performance of "Romeo and Juliet," the Opera Association reserved a block of 1200 tickets at special rates for high school English, drama, speech, and music classes. Teachers were provided notes discussing the differences in the Shakespearean interpretation and Gounod's musical representation of the story. A great success!

The activities in the above described cities have met or are meeting with tremendous success. The single most significant change is that the cultural organizations and the business and lay community leaders concerned with cultural activities have begun thinking "educationally" in terms of developing programs.

REFERENCES

1. Haney, William R. "Enrichment of The Culture Life of the Student Beyond The Traditional School Program." Unpublished Master's Thesis, Texas Christian University, Fort Worth, 1966.

2. Green, George. On Special Assignment to the Curriculum Office, School District of Philadelphia. Personal correspondence of William R. Haney, December 6, 1965.

3. Willis, Benjamin C. *Compensatory Education in Chicago Public Schools.* Chicago: Chicago Public Schools, 1964.

4. Shepard, Samuel, Jr., Assistant Superintendent, Banneker Group of Schools, St. Louis, Missouri. Personal correspondence of William R. Haney, December 6, 1965.

5. Mitchell, Charles. "The Culturally Deprived—A Matter of Concern." Detroit: Detroit Public Schools, 1965. (Mimeographed.)

6. *San Diego Zoo Educational Programs.* A Community Educational Resources Publication. San Diego: Department of Education, San Diego County, 1964.

7. "Project Change." Title III ESEA Application for Continuation for Grant #OEG-7-8-005360-0048-(056), Fort Worth. Education Service Center, Region XI, April 1969.

84